Canada Close Up

P9-AQR-210

Manitoba

GREAT WHITE BEAR TOURS

Rachel Eagen

Scholastic Canada Ltd.

Toronto   New York   London   Auckland   S
Mexico City   New Delhi   Hong Kong   Buen

Visual Credits

p. I: Blaine Harrington/age fotostock/Maxx Images; p. III: Dave Reede/All Canada Photos; p. IV: (middle left) Jack Cronkhite/Shutterstock Inc., (top right) Dennis Donohue/Shutterstock Inc.; pp. 2-3 and back cover: Dave Reede/All Canada Photos; p. 3: John Henshall/Alamy; p. 4: (bottom) Thorsten Milse/Maxx Images; p. 5: Taylor S. Kennedy/National Geographic Stock; p. 6: Terrance Klassen/Alamy; p. 7: Ron Garnett/AirScapes.ca; p. 8: (top) Bill Brooks/Alamy, (bottom) Serg Zastavkin/Shutterstock Inc.; p. 9: Mike Grandmaison/Corbis; p. 10: (top) Daryl Benson/Masterfile, (bottom) Ken Gigliotti/Winnipeg Free Press, 07-23-08; p. 11: (top) Thorsten Milse/Robert Harding World Imagery/Corbis, (bottom) Thorsten Milse/Maxx Images; p. 12: H.L. Hime/Library and Archives Canada/C-016447; p. 13: (top) Library and Archives Canada, Acc. No. 1989-492-2, (bottom) Karl Bodmer/Glenbow Archives; p. 14: Glenbow Archives; p. 15: (all) North Wind/North Wind Picture Archives; p. 16: North Wind/North Wind Picture Archives; p. 17: Glenbow Archives; p. 18: Library and Archives Canada, Copyright Canada Post Corporation; p. 19: Archives of Manitoba, M.A. McLeod 1 (N10612); p. 21: Glenbow Archives; p. 22: Glenbow Archives; p. 23: Library and Archives Canada/PA-163001; p. 24: McCord Museum MP-0000.1421.8; p. 25: Ken Gigliotti/Winnipeg Free Press/CP Images, p. 26: (top) William Kurelek, *Manitoba Party*, 1964, photo © National Gallery of Canada, National Gallery of Canada, Ottawa, (bottom) ShyMan/iStockPhoto; p. 27: Joe Bryksa/Winnipeg Free Press/CP Images; p. 28: jonpeters/Alamy; p. 29: (top) Keith Levit/Alamy, (bottom) The Canadian Press/John Woods; p. 30: (top) Keith Levit/Alamy, (bottom) The Canadian Press/Adrian Wyld; p. 31: (top) CanuckStock/Shutterstock Inc., (bottom) Falk Kienas/Shutterstock Inc.; p. 32: Photo courtesy of Amy Miller/New Flyer Industries Canada; p. 33: Brian Milne/First Light; p. 34: Christopher Morris/Corbis; p. 35: (top) Martine Oger/Shutterstock Inc., (bottom left) Dmitry Kosterev/Shutterstock Inc., (bottom right) Melinda Fawver/First Light; p. 36: Mike Grandmaison/AllCanadaPhotos.com; p. 37: (top) Mike Rogal/Shutterstock Inc., (bottom) Route66/Shutterstock Inc.; p. 39: Dave Reede/AllCanadaPhotos.com; p. 40: Inland Waters Directorate/Library and Archives Canada/e002343918; p. 41: Terrance Klassen/Alamy; p. 42: Barrett & MacKay/AllCanadaPhotos.com; p. 43: (top) Bettmann/Corbis, (bottom) McDermid studio, Edmonton, Alberta/Glenbow Archives.

Produced by Plan B Book Packagers
Editorial: Ellen Rodger
Design: Rosie Gowsell-Pattison
Editor: Jon Eben Field
Special thanks to consultant and editor Terrance Cox, adjunct professor, Brock University; Tanya Rutledge and Jim Chernishenko.

Library and Archives Canada Cataloguing in Publication

Eagen, Rachel, 1979-
Manitoba / Rachel Eagen.
(Canada close up)
ISBN 978-0-545-98903-9

1. Manitoba--Juvenile literature.
I. Title. II. Series: Canada close up (Toronto, Ont.)
FC3361.2.E34 2009   j971.27   C2009-900237-X

ISBN-10 0-545-98903-5

6 5 4 3 2 1   Printed in Canada   09 10 11 12 13 14

Contents

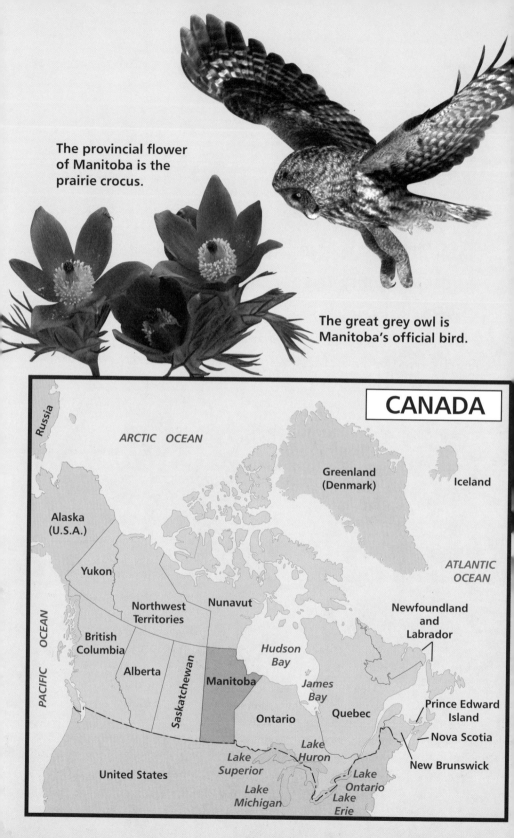

The provincial flower of Manitoba is the prairie crocus.

The great grey owl is Manitoba's official bird.

CANADA

Russia

ARCTIC OCEAN

Greenland (Denmark)

Iceland

Alaska (U.S.A.)

ATLANTIC OCEAN

Yukon

Nunavut

Newfoundland and Labrador

Northwest Territories

PACIFIC OCEAN

British Columbia

Hudson Bay

Alberta

Saskatchewan

Manitoba

James Bay

Ontario

Quebec

Prince Edward Island

Nova Scotia

Lake Huron

New Brunswick

United States

Lake Superior

Lake Ontario

Lake Michigan

Lake Erie

Welcome to Manitoba!

Say Manitoba and some people picture wide-open prairies with rolling fields of golden wheat. Some may imagine a wilderness of forests and rocky barrens. For others, Manitoba brings to mind the historic fur trade, polar bears or marauding mosquitoes.

The province has a long and fascinating past. The word Manitoba is thought to have come from the Cree words *manitou bou* – "the narrows of the Great Spirit." Settlement here opened up the Canadian west. It is the homeland of the Métis, a people whose history is both European and Aboriginal.

Manitoba's many lakes and rivers have shaped its history and economy. It has an arctic seaport at Churchill and the largest inland fishing industry in the country. Manitoba is many things!

Chapter 1
The Keystone Province

Manitoba is sometimes called "the **keystone** province" because it is located in the middle of the country. It is considered one of the prairie provinces, along with Saskatchewan and Alberta, because in the south the land is flat and the climate dry. But Manitoba also has thousands of freshwater lakes, arctic shrub lands and large forests that stretch across rocky regions in the centre and north.

Prairie and forest

Manitobans pride themselves on being friendly. It even says so on their licence plates!

The prairie makes up about one-third of Manitoba, and stretches across the southern region of the province. The flat landscape and rich soil make this region ideal for agriculture. These former grasslands yield crops of wheat, oats, barley, canola and flax. Winnipeg, the provincial capital, is located on the prairie, as are many of Manitoba's larger cities, such as Brandon, Portage la Prairie and Steinbach.

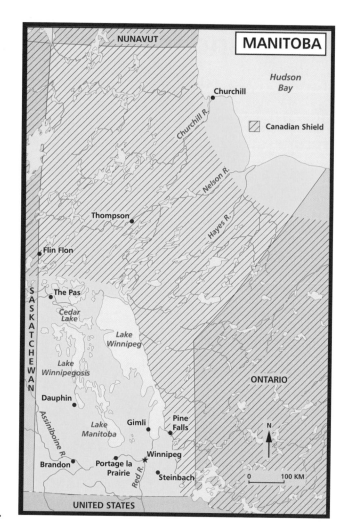

MANITOBA

NUNAVUT

Hudson Bay

Churchill

Churchill R.

Nelson R.

Canadian Shield

Thompson

Hayes R.

Flin Flon

The Pas

S A S K A T C H E W A N

Cedar Lake

Lake Winnipeg

Lake Winnipegosis

ONTARIO

Dauphin

Lake Manitoba

Gimli

Pine Falls

N

Assiniboine R.

Brandon

Portage la Prairie

Red R.

Winnipeg

Steinbach

0   100 KM

UNITED STATES

Foxes live in Manitoba's boreal forests.

Large boreal forests tower over the landscape throughout central Manitoba. **Evergreens**, such as white and black spruce, fir and jack pine grow here, along with **deciduous** trees, including oak, aspen, elm, ash and Manitoba maple. Moose, elk, caribou, deer, and fur-bearing animals such as black bears, timber wolves, foxes, otters, bobcats, minks and lynx live in the forests. Pockets of bogs and marshes are also common in the forested areas, and are home to wildlife such as beaver and muskrat.

Black spruce grows in the bogs of Manitoba's north-central boreal forest.

Swimmers and sunbathers flock to Lake Winnipeg's Grand Beach in the summer.

Rivers and lakes

There are more than 100,000 freshwater lakes of varying sizes in Manitoba. Lake Winnipeg, the largest lake in the province, is the fifth-largest freshwater lake in Canada. It covers 24,514 square kilometres from central Manitoba almost to Winnipeg. The white sand beaches of Grand Beach Provincial Park run for three kilometres along its eastern shore. Cedar Lake, Lake Winnipegosis and Lake Manitoba link together, stretching from central to southern Manitoba.

Hudson Bay, in the northeast, is an inland sea joined to the Arctic Ocean. The Hudson Bay Lowlands are cool climate wetlands where many species of birds nest each summer. As ways to travel, the Red, Assiniboine, Nelson, Churchill, Hayes and Whiteshell rivers were very important to the early settlement of the province. Now their rushing waters are a major source of hydroelectric power.

The Assiniboine River flows through Winnipeg and joins the Red River at The Forks.

The city of Flin Flon was built on the rocks of the Canadian Shield. It has an above-ground heated water and sewage system encased in wooden boxes.

Rocks and ice

The rocks of the Canadian Shield emerge in central Manitoba and extend to the north. This ancient **geological** formation is an important source of minerals and metals. In the far north of the province, an area known as the taiga is home to caribou, arctic fox and wolverine. Trees grow only sparsely in this area and winters are harsh and long.

The wolverine is well-adapted to living in cold regions.

Snow and hoarfrost cling to trees on a prairie farm.

Sunny skies and snow

Manitoba is one of the sunniest provinces in
Canada. The skies are often clear and
cloudless, especially in the southern regions.
But blizzards in winter and tornadoes in
summer are common in the south too. There
are extreme differences between summer and
winter in Manitoba. The summers are hot
and humid, and the winters are very cold.
The entire province receives heavy snowfall
during the winter months.

A giant mosquito sculpture stands in the town of Komarno. The town's name is the Ukrainian word for mosquito.

Mosquito weather

Manitoba is known as the mosquito capital of Canada because the insects here are annoying and plentiful. The province's many lakes and springtime river floods make ideal breeding grounds. Manitobans often joke that the mosquito is the province's official bird.

Fishflies cling to a wall. The insects swarm towns and cities around Manitoba's many lakes each summer.

The polar bear capital

Each fall, when the cold weather settles on the shores of Hudson Bay, the northern town of Churchill becomes a popular spot for tourists from around the world. They come to see the town's most famous visitors: polar bears.

The 600-kilogram bears hunt for seals on the frozen bay waters. Sightseeing tours venture onto the ice in tundra buggies – vehicles with massive tires that won't slip or slide. The curious bears come almost nose-to-nose with the tourists.

Chapter 2
Like Nowhere Else

One hundred and fifty years ago, Manitoba was a fur-trading territory. Its people were hunters and fur traders: the Aboriginal peoples of the plains and woodlands, and the Métis, who were the descendants of European fur traders and Aboriginal women.

The Métis were bison hunters who lived between two cultures.

Bison meat was dried for later use and hauled on big-wheeled carts called Red River carts.

On the land

Aboriginal peoples have lived in Manitoba for over 12,000 years. Their descendants include the Inuit in the far north who hunted caribou, seals and whales near the coast of Hudson Bay. The Chipewyan in the northwest, and the Ojibwa and Cree in central Manitoba, hunted caribou, moose and elk. They also gathered fruits and berries in the boreal forests. The Assiniboine peoples lived on the southern prairie, following and hunting the great herds of bison.

The Assiniboine wore clothing made from bison hides.

York boats could carry up to six tonnes of cargo and were used by the Hudson's Bay Company during the fur trade.

Exploration

The first Europeans to venture into Manitoba were explorers searching for the Northwest Passage, a sea route through Arctic waters to the riches of China. In 1610, Henry Hudson sailed from England and followed the Arctic Ocean to the bay that was later named after him – Hudson Bay. The search for the Northwest Passage brought other European explorers to Churchill, which in 1717 became a fur trading post.

The fur trade was a major industry in North America from the 1600s until the late 1800s. In 1670 King Charles II of England granted an enormous territory to a new trading company called the Hudson's Bay Company (HBC).

Hudson Bay was named for Henry Hudson, the English explorer who first navigated the shores of the great bay.

The territory, which included all of Manitoba, most of Saskatchewan, and parts of northern Quebec, Ontario and Alberta, was called Rupert's Land. The Hudson's Bay Company had sole control over this territory. It set up forts and sent out more explorers to establish trading relations with the Aboriginal peoples.

Samuel Hearne was an English explorer for the Hudson's Bay Company. He travelled in northern Manitoba and traced the Coppermine River to the Arctic.

Fur trade rivalries

The Hudson's Bay Company traded in Rupert's Land with little competition for 100 years. In 1794 the North West Company sent **canoe brigades** of *voyageurs*, or French fur traders, from Montreal to Fort William on the shores of Lake Superior. Fort William became an exchange point where Aboriginal trappers and Métis suppliers from Rupert's Land met to trade with *voyageurs*.

This challenged the Hudson's Bay Company **monopoly**. The two companies were bitter rivals. They fought over territory and competed for Aboriginal trading partners.

Voyageurs made their way to Fort William using rivers and lakes as highways.

The Métis

The Métis are a distinct Aboriginal people who have their origins in the fur trade. European fur traders often had Aboriginal wives, and their children became known as Métis. On the plains, the Métis were bison hunters and fur traders. They lived in a culture that mixed European and Aboriginal customs and many spoke French in addition to Aboriginal languages. Métis hunters supplied the North West Company with pemmican, an important, high-energy food source for *voyageurs*. Pemmican was made from dried bison meat, fat and berries. It was easy to transport and used to make stews.

The Métis adapted French ox carts to transport bison carcasses during hunts. Known as Red River carts, they could carry 400 kilograms and were made entirely of wood and leather. The cartwheels made ear-piercing squeals as they turned.

The Red River Colony

Lord Selkirk was a **shareholder** in the Hudson's Bay Company. In 1812 he was granted HBC land for a settlement of Scottish immigrants on the Red and Assiniboine rivers. Called the Red River Colony, it was unstable from the start. Settlers lacked farming equipment and food was scarce. And the North West Company's pemmican supply line was blocked by the settlement.

With food in short supply, Lord Selkirk banned settlers from taking food outside the colony. This angered the Métis, who considered the colony within their territory.

Lord Selkirk used his wealth and power to try to dominate the fur trade in Manitoba, through the Red River Colony and the HBC.

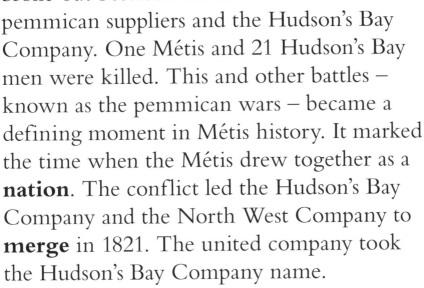

Métis fur trader Cuthbert Grant worked for the North West Company. He led the Métis in the Battle of Seven Oaks and later established a town named Grantown on the Assiniboine River.

The North West Company tried to convince the colony's settlers to move. In 1816, at Seven Oaks, a battle broke out between Métis pemmican suppliers and the Hudson's Bay Company. One Métis and 21 Hudson's Bay men were killed. This and other battles – known as the pemmican wars – became a defining moment in Métis history. It marked the time when the Métis drew together as a **nation**. The conflict led the Hudson's Bay Company and the North West Company to **merge** in 1821. The united company took the Hudson's Bay Company name.

The settlers of the Red River Colony limped through bad weather, poor crops and floods. In 1836, sixteen years after Selkirk's death, his family transferred the colony back to the Hudson's Bay Company. By the 1860s the Métis outnumbered the Scottish settlers.

Confederation and resistance

Nova Scotia, New Brunswick, Ontario and Quebec joined together in **Confederation** in 1867. The new country of Canada wanted more territory and began negotiating with the Hudson Bay's Company for Rupert's Land. The people of the Red River Colony, including the Métis, were never consulted. When Rupert's Land was transferred to Canada in 1869 and called the Northwest Territories, the Métis tried to ensure their place in the new country.

Led by Louis Riel, they formed a **provisional** government and drew up a list of rights. The government hoped to form a province. Many English-speaking settlers in Red River opposed the Métis government and this led to the **Red River Resistance**.

During the Resistance, Riel's government executed an English prisoner, Thomas Scott, after he plotted against the Métis provisional government. Scott's death angered the rest of the country and forced Riel into **exile**. Manitoba became a province in 1870, and most of the Métis list of rights was made law.

In 1806 Marie-Anne Gaboury came from Quebec with her *voyageur* husband, Jean-Baptiste Lagimodière. She was Louis Riel's grandmother and the first woman of European descent to settle in Manitoba.

Northwest Resistance

After the Red River Resistance, many Métis moved to Saskatchewan, then still part of the Northwest Territories. When the bison began to disappear from over-hunting, and new settlers from Ontario trickled in, the Métis again feared a loss of territory.

They asked Louis Riel to return from exile to represent them in an appeal to the Canadian government. When that failed, they organized the Northwest Resistance in 1885. The Resistance was unsuccessful. Many Métis and their First Nations allies were killed or surrendered and were put on trial and sentenced to prison or death.

Riel – father of a nation

In Manitoba, Louis Riel is considered a founder of the province. Riel was born at the Red River Colony in 1844 and educated in Montreal. He was a leader, an elected politician, a rebel and a visionary who saw a future for his people in a province with an elected government. Riel led his people in two resistance movements. He was tried for **treason** and executed in Saskatchewan in 1885. Riel's death was **controversial**. In English Canada, Riel was viewed as a traitor and a murderer. In French Canada, he was seen as a champion of French rights and culture.

Growing pains

Manitoba's boundaries and population grew after it became a province. Nearly 45,000 immigrants arrived between 1870 and 1881 on the newly built Canadian Pacific Railway. These European immigrants built farms or settled in the growing cities.

In 1919 Winnipeg was the scene of the country's best-known labour strike. The Winnipeg General Strike saw 35,000 people walk off the job to protest low wages and poor working conditions. Factories and stores closed. Firefighters, postal workers and telephone operators left their jobs too. The whole city ground to a halt. The strike ended after ten days when the Royal Canadian Mounted Police beat back a crowd of strikers and the leaders were arrested.

The Great Depression (1929-1939) was a time of hardship in Manitoba. **Drought** ruined grain crops on the prairie. In the cities, many people were out of work. The hard times ended with the beginning of World War II. After the war, Manitoba's mining and lumber towns boomed and farming recovered.

The Winnipeg General Strike in 1919 ended after ten days.

This Mennonite farming homestead in southern Manitoba represents the life of many European immigrants who came to the province in the late 1800s and early 1900s.

Chapter 3
From Far and Wide

Manitoba's 1,196,000 residents come from many backgrounds and cultures. The eastern European immigrants who settled here in the late 1800s were followed by waves of people from other parts of Europe. Many were escaping poverty or oppression in their homelands. They brought their food, music and ways of life to their new homes.

A group of people dress like Vikings during the Icelandic Festival of Manitoba.

Vikings and Mennonites

Fleeing volcanic eruptions in their homeland, thousands of people from Iceland settled near Lake Winnipeg in the 1870s. They established the Republic of New Iceland in Gimli, by the shores of Lake Winnipeg, from 1876 to 1887. Nearly 27,000 people of Icelandic heritage still live in Manitoba. Every summer since 1932 an Icelandic festival has been held at Gimli.

The Mennonites, a German–speaking Christian group, fled religious **persecution** in Europe in the 1870s. Thousands settled in southern Manitoba and built farm communities such as Steinbach and Altona.

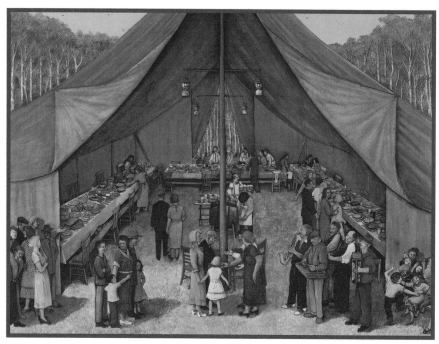
Ukrainian-Canadian painter William Kurelek depicted a prairie wedding celebration in this colourful oil painting.

Ukrainian immigrants set up farming communities in Manitoba in the late 1800s. Ukrainian culture has influenced Manitoba in many ways. Perogies, which are potato and cheese dumplings, are common on many Manitoba restaurant menus. The National Ukrainian Festival is held every August in the city of Dauphin. It includes performances of traditional Ukrainian dance, as well as music and food.

Festivals and parties

Dozens of different cultural festivals make the Manitoba calendar lively. Folklorama, held in Winnipeg each August, is by far the largest. This two-week festival is a celebration of Manitoba's ethnic heritages. In February, *le Festival du Voyageur* is held in St. Boniface, the largest French-speaking community in Manitoba. The festival is a celebration of the *voyageurs* who worked in the early fur trade. Concerts featuring French-Canadian music are the main attraction of this festival.

Sled dogs race in a competition at *le Festival du Voyageur* in St. Boniface.

Paraguayan dancers perform at Winnipeg's Folklorama Festival, which celebrates multiculturalism.

The Northern Manitoba Trappers' Festival in The Pas celebrates fur trapping, which is still a source of income for people in northern communities. Festival events include dogsled racing, chainsaw cutting and a beard-growing contest where participants earn prizes for the shaggiest beard or the best moustache!

One event that is unique to the province is the Manitoba social. Socials are big community parties that have their roots in pioneer Ukrainian wedding celebrations.

Today Manitoba socials involve food, drink, music, dance and games such as bingo or cards. Tickets are sold for admission to a social, and guests must also buy tickets for food and beverages. The money raised goes to a community cause or a young couple about to get married.

The Golden Boy stands atop the Manitoba Legislative Building in Winnipeg. He faces north, holding a sheaf of wheat and raising a torch to the province's natural resources.

Two women buy raffle tickets at a 1980s-themed wedding social.

Prairie winds make Winnipeg feel even colder in winter.

Winnipeg

Manitoba's capital city is known for its long, cold and snowy winters. Its nickname is Winterpeg. Situated at the forks of the Red and Assiniboine rivers, in the province's south, Winnipeg has many historic and cultural sites, including Fort Garry, a former Hudson's Bay Company trading post. Canada's oldest ballet company, the Royal Winnipeg Ballet, was founded here in 1939. Winnipeg is home to the Canadian Football League's Winnipeg Blue Bombers, ten-time winners of the Grey Cup. Bomber fans often paint their faces blue and gold – the team's colours.

Bannock and jambusters

Each fall, southern Manitoba communities host harvest suppers. Held in church and community halls, the suppers evolved from "fowl suppers," feasts held in duck or goose hunting season. Today, harvest suppers raise funds for community projects

Jam busters

and feature roast turkey, Ukrainian cabbage rolls and **Hutterite** air rolls. Air rolls are homemade dinner rolls that are smooth and airy. Other Manitoban treats include jambusters – jelly-filled powdered doughnuts – and *ponnukokur*, Icelandic pancakes rolled in brown sugar. Bannock is a type of grilled quick bread adapted from Scottish settler recipes and made by the Métis. Bannock dough is sometimes combined with dried fruits and fried into what are called Red River twists.

Fried bannock

Chapter 4
Making a Living

Manitoba is rich in natural resources and good farmland. Mineral deposits in the Canadian Shield, which covers the upper half of the province, support mines that produce nickel, copper, gold and zinc. The long, mighty rivers of Manitoba are harnessed as a source of hydroelectric power. Fields of grain and sunflowers grow on the southern prairies.

But Manitoba's economy is not just resource-based. Manufacturing is the largest economic engine in the province, with factories producing rocket motors, furniture, windows, doors and processed foods. The buses that transport many urban North Americans to work were most likely built in Manitoba.

New Flyer, based in Winnipeg, is the largest manufacturer of transit buses in Canada and the United States. The company also makes new fuel-efficient buses.

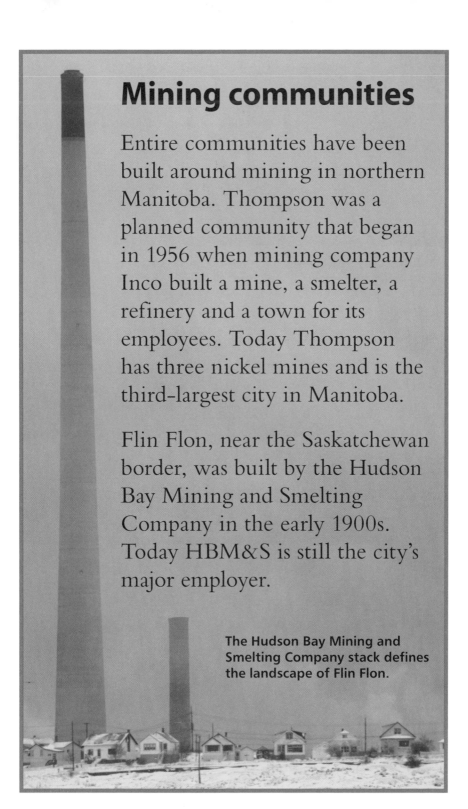

Mining communities

Entire communities have been built around mining in northern Manitoba. Thompson was a planned community that began in 1956 when mining company Inco built a mine, a smelter, a refinery and a town for its employees. Today Thompson has three nickel mines and is the third-largest city in Manitoba.

Flin Flon, near the Saskatchewan border, was built by the Hudson Bay Mining and Smelting Company in the early 1900s. Today HBM&S is still the city's major employer.

The Hudson Bay Mining and Smelting Company stack defines the landscape of Flin Flon.

Manitoba's Jenpeg Generating Station and dam on the Nelson River create power for the province.

A hydroelectric powerhouse

Much of the power generated in the province comes from rivers in the north. The hydroelectric power is more than enough for Manitoba's needs. The **surplus** is sold to Saskatchewan and Ontario.

One of the major hydroelectric power plants is built on the Nelson River. The Nelson River Hydroelectric Project provides the province with power and a major source of income. But the construction of a huge dam resulted in the flooding of large areas of land where First Nations communities lived. Some lost their traditional hunting and trapping areas while others were forced to relocate permanently.

Trees, trapping and fishing

The boreal forests of central Manitoba are important to the economy. Trees are cut and processed to make furniture and paper and to build homes. The Pas and Pine Falls are important mill towns in Manitoba.

Woodland animals such as bear, fox, coyote, beaver, moose, caribou and elk are hunted and trapped for their furs and pelts. Trapping animals is a controversial issue today, and trappers in Manitoba face pressure from animal rights groups to stop. Trapping is a way of life for many Aboriginal peoples in northern Manitoba.

Manitoba's many lakes support an unusual fishing industry: fly-in fishing camps and lodges. Walleye, northern pike and trout are common lake fish caught by sport fishers. The largest inland fishing industry in Canada is on Lake Winnipeg. Fishing fleets haul in good catches of pickerel, whitefish, perch and goldeye, among other species.

The sunflower province

Agriculture has always been important in Manitoba. The main crop is wheat, but other crops are also important, like flax seed, oats, barley, canola, buckwheat and sunflowers. In fact, Manitoba is the country's biggest producer of sunflower and flax seeds. Sugar beets and potatoes, and legumes such as lentils, are grown on a smaller scale.

Meat and dairy are also part of the agricultural industry in Manitoba, but they are not as important as the grain crops. However, Manitoba has the largest hog-farming industry in Canada, producing over nine million pigs a year.

A farmer examines his wheat crop at harvest time.

The Royal Canadian Mint

The Winnipeg branch of the Royal Canadian Mint opened in 1976. The mint makes millions of coins every year! It also produces coins for 100 countries around the world. Visitors to the mint can watch the coins being pressed, and see rare, handcrafted coins on display. The mint also specializes in coins commemorating events such as the Olympic Games.

Chapter 5
The Mighty Red

The Red River looms large in the history of Manitoba. It was a major route used by French and English fur traders and later became the site of Lord Selkirk's Red River Colony. The river's source, or starting point, is Lake Traverse, in North Dakota. It flows northward between North Dakota and Minnesota and into the Red River Valley and Winnipeg, before ending in Lake Winnipeg. About 249 of the river's 885 kilometres flow through Manitoba.

The great floods

People who live near the Red River talk about the river's many floods. Spring floods are common, especially after winters with heavy snowfall. This is why many river communities have dikes to protect them from rising waters. The biggest floods in recent memory happened in 1950, 1997 and 2009.

The flooded Red River made a lake of roads and farms in 1997.

Houses were swamped during the 1950 flood and thousands had to flee. This led to the construction of a floodway.

In 1950 dikes protecting Winnipeg gave way and water overwhelmed much of the city. Almost 70,000 people were evacuated by the Canadian army. Four of the city's eleven bridges were destroyed. In 1997, the river flooded a huge area from North Dakota to Winnipeg. In southern Manitoba, the flood waters crested at a height of 7.5 metres.

The floodway

The 1950 flood caused over $100 million in damage. The provincial government decided to build a floodway to prevent future floods from destroying property. The Red River Floodway was completed in 1968.

This 47-kilometre system includes a long, deep channel for floodwaters to empty, as well as a network of dikes and dams that divert waters and prevent them from spilling over Winnipeg and the surrounding communities.

In 1997 an emergency dike was built as a result of warnings that another disastrous flood was coming. The project, known as the Brunkild Z-Dike, is believed to have saved the city of Winnipeg by a hair. Unfortunately, rural communities weren't so lucky. About 200,000 hectares of farmland were swamped and 28,000 people were evacuated. The land was so saturated that the waters took several months to drain.

In 2005 work began on an expansion of the Red River Floodway, to be completed in 2010.

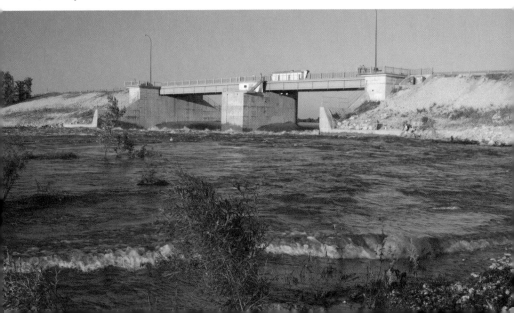

Chapter 6

Points of Pride

▶ The International Peace Garden spans the American–Canadian border between North Dakota and Manitoba. The 947-hectare garden includes a floral clock, fountains and a peace chapel. It commemorates veterans of the First and Second World Wars, as well as the victims of 9/11, and celebrates individuals committed to peace.

▶ Red River Cereal is a hot cereal made of wheat, rye and flax. It originated in St. Boniface, Manitoba, in 1924.

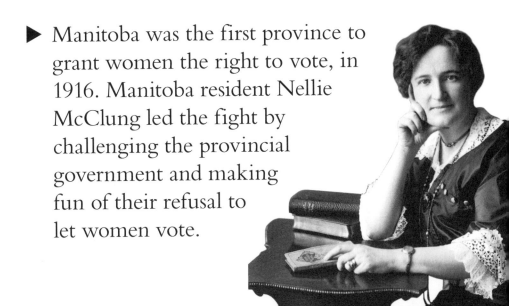

► Former National Hockey League star Bobby Clarke, from Flin Flon, played his entire career with the Philadelphia Flyers. A Hockey Hall of Fame member, Clarke won the league's Most Valuable Player trophy three times and was voted one of the top 100 players of all time.

► Thompson, in northern Manitoba, is a testing area for North American car manufacturers. The subarctic climate means carmakers can test vehicles in real cold-weather situations.

► Manitoba was the first province to grant women the right to vote, in 1916. Manitoba resident Nellie McClung led the fight by challenging the provincial government and making fun of their refusal to let women vote.

Glossary

canoe brigades: Groups or fleets travelling to the same post

Confederation: The joining of New Brunswick, Nova Scotia, Ontario and Quebec in 1867 to form the Dominion of Canada

controversial: Causing debate and disagreement

deciduous: Describes a tree or shrub that sheds leaves in the fall

drought: A long period without rainfall

evergreens: Trees or shrubs that keep their leaves throughout the year

exile: Banishment from one's native land

geological: Dealing with the physical structure of the Earth

Hutterite: Refers to a Christian group, originally from Europe, who live communally

keystone: The central stone of an arch; the central principle

merge: Join or combine

monopoly: Exclusive control of trade

nation: A group of people with a common history and language

persecution: Ill treatment because of race or beliefs

provisional: Temporary

Red River Resistance: A series of negotiations and confrontations (1869-1870) between the newly formed Canadian government and the Métis of the Red River Colony

shareholder: An owner of shares in a company

surplus: The excess, or amount left over

treason: An attempt to overthrow one's own ruler or government